JEB
STUART

Other titles in *Historical American Biographies*

Annie Oakley
Legendary Sharpshooter
ISBN 0-7660-1012-0

John Wesley Powell
Explorer of the Grand Canyon
ISBN 0-89490-783-2

Benjamin Franklin
Founding Father and Inventor
ISBN 0-89490-784-0

Lewis and Clark
Explorers of the Northwest
ISBN 0-7660-1016-3

Buffalo Bill Cody
Western Legend
ISBN 0-7660-1015-5

Martha Washington
First Lady
ISBN 0-7660-1017-1

Clara Barton
Civil War Nurse
ISBN 0-89490-778-6

Paul Revere
Rider for the Revolution
ISBN 0-89490-779-4

Jeb Stuart
Confederate Cavalry General
ISBN 0-7660-1013-9

Robert E. Lee
Southern Hero of the Civil War
ISBN 0-89490-782-4

Jefferson Davis
President of the Confederacy
ISBN 0-7660-1064-3

Stonewall Jackson
Confederate General
ISBN 0-89490-781-6

Jesse James
Legendary Outlaw
ISBN 0-7660-1055-4

Susan B. Anthony
Voice for Women's Voting Rights
ISBN 0-89490-780-8

Thomas Alva Edison
Inventor
ISBN 0-7660-1014-7

Historical American Biographies

JEB STUART

Confederate Cavalry General

Lynda Pflueger

Enslow Publishers, Inc.

44 Fadem Road   PO Box 38
Box 699   Aldershot
Springfield, NJ 07081   Hants GU12 6BP
USA   UK

Dedication
To my critique group: Alison, Barbara, Kathy, and Lois.

Library of Congress Cataloging-in-Publication Data

Pflueger, Lynda.
    Jeb Stuart: Confederate cavalry general / Lynda Pflueger.
       p. cm. — (Historical American biographies)
    Includes bibliographical references (p.) and index.
    Summary: Traces the life of the famous Confederate general from his
childhood in Virginia through his West Point education and brilliant
military career to his death following the Battle of Yellow Tavern.
    ISBN 0-7660-1013-9
    1. Stuart, Jeb, 1833–1864—Juvenile literature. 2. Generals—
Confederate States of America—Biography—Juvenile literature.
3. Confederate States of America. Army—Biography—Juvenile
literature. 4. United States—History—Civil War, 1861–1865—Cavalry
operations—Juvenile literature. [1. Stuart, Jeb, 1833–1864.
2. Generals. 3. United States—History—Civil War, 1861–1865.]
I. Title. II. Series.
E467.1.S9P48 1998
973.7'42—dc21
                                    97-4367
                                      CIP
                                      AC

Printed in the United States of America

10 9 8 7 6 5 4 3 2 1

Illustration Credits: Enslow Publishers, Inc., pp. 14, 101; Kansas State
Historical Society, Topeka, Kansas, p. 34; Library of Congress, pp. 6, 42,
46, 114; Massachusetts Commandery Military Order of the Loyal
Legion and the U.S. Army Military History Institute, pp. 12, 50, 55, 61,
86, 110; Virginia Historical Society, Richmond, Virginia, p. 24; Special
Collections Division of the United States Military Academy Library,
West Point, New York, p. 22; The Museum of the Confederacy,
Richmond, Virginia, photography by Katherine Wetzel, p. 75; National
Archives, p. 63, 102.

Cover Illustration: Corel (Background); Library of Congress (Inset).

CONTENTS

1 Scout and Raider. 7

2 Young Stuart 16

3 The Frontier 26

4 John Brown's Raid 37

5 Civil War 44

6 Stuart's Cavalry 54

7 The Battlefield in 1862 67

8 The Battlefield in 1863 85

9 Stuart's Last Battle 104

10 Epilogue 113

Chronology 117

Chapter Notes 118

Glossary 124

Further Reading 126

Index 127

James Ewell Brown (Jeb) Stuart liked to wear a gray coat lined in red silk, golden spurs, an ostrich feather in his hat, and white buckskin gloves. Despite his showy appearance, he took his command seriously.

1

SCOUT AND RAIDER

In the spring of 1862, the Union Army under command of General George B. McClellan was preparing to strike the Confederate capital of Richmond. McClellan's goal was to end the Civil War with one major battle. Instead of taking his army over land, he chose to float his forces down the Potomac River to Fort Monroe. The fort was located between the York and James rivers on the tip of the Virginia Peninsula. From there, he would march his army up the peninsula to Richmond. "I will bring you face to face with the rebels," McClellan promised his men.[1]

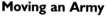

Moving an Army
It took three weeks to move McClellan's army, and 400 ships to transport 121,500 men, 14,952 horses and mules, 1,150 wagons, 44 artillery batteries, 74 ambulances, pontoon bridges, provisions for all the men and livestock, tents, and telegraph wire.[2]

Slowly and cautiously, McClellan worked his way up the peninsula until he was only five miles from Richmond. His army was spread out for over twenty miles along the Chickahominy River. He brought up his big guns, 101 pieces of artillery, and planned to blast his way into the town.

Outnumbered and outgunned, General Robert E. Lee, commander of the Confederate forces, devised a bold plan to save the capital. He hoped to pull McClellan's attention away from Richmond by attacking his army's most vulnerable point.

Stuart's Orders

Suspecting that the right flank of McClellan's army was unprotected, Lee sent his cavalry commander, Colonel James Ewell Brown Stuart, on a scouting expedition. Lee ordered Stuart to explore the territory occupied by McClellan's right flank and report back its location and numbers. Stuart was also ordered to disrupt the Union Army's supply and communication lines.

After receiving his orders, Stuart selected twelve hundred horsemen to accompany him on his raid. At two o'clock in the morning on June 12, he awakened them by announcing, "Gentlemen, in ten minutes every man must be in his saddle!"[3] He told no one his destination. Many of the men thought they were going to the Shenandoah Valley to join Stonewall Jackson's army.

It turned into a sweltering, muggy day as they rode steadily northward. At Turner's Tavern they veered left and crossed over the Richmond, Fredericksburg, and Potomac railroad tracks. By nightfall they had traveled twenty-two miles and camped a few miles north of Ashland, Virginia. They lit no campfires so their location would not be apparent.

At first light on June 13, flares were sent up to signal the beginning of the day's march. They were too close to the enemy for bugles to be sounded. As they traveled in an easterly direction, it soon became apparent that they were not headed for the Shenandoah Valley. At this point Stuart informed several of his key commanders of his orders.

Hanover Court House

Stuart sent scouts out ahead of the main body of men. Later that morning, the scouts reported sighting

Union cavalry, about one hundred fifty men, up ahead at Hanover Court House. Stuart dispatched Fitzhugh Lee and his men to go around the town and block the Union cavalry's retreat. He did not want them to sound an alarm. Then he marched forward to confront them. The Northern horsemen chose to flee instead of fight. Due to the swampy terrain, Lee's men were unable to intercept them.

Stuart continued to move forward cautiously. He knew that an attack by Union troops, at this point, would delay his march and jeopardize his mission. Carefully he approached a bridge over Totopotomoy Creek. Union horsemen were nearby, but they simply watched the Confederates as they crossed. A mile from the bridge, however, the Union troops decided to take a stand. One hundred Union horsemen stood on the crest of a hill, ready for battle.

"Form fours! Draw sabers! Charge!" Stuart ordered.[4] Four abreast they attacked, yelling and waving their sabers. Their sudden assault overcame the Union troopers, who scattered in confusion. The Union cavalry fell back toward their camp in the village of Old Church. A mile before they reached the village, the Union troops received reinforcements and again formed a battle line. Stuart's men charged and broke through it. Finally, the battle reached the Union camp and the Confederate horsemen destroyed it.

Courthouses

Williamsburg and Yorktown were the main towns on the Virginia Peninsula. Because of the long distance between them, courthouses were built at Hanover, Charles City, and New Kent. The courthouses served as gathering places for local citizens and became focal points on the country roads of the region.

At this point Stuart had to decide whether to go back the way he had come or ride completely around McClellan's army. He had obtained the information he needed. The right flank of the Union Army was unprotected and vulnerable to attack, but he feared that if he returned the same way he had come, he would call attention to that fact. Keeping his uncertainty to himself, he decided to continue his circuit around the Union Army.

He ordered his column to move forward. Realizing they were in great danger, one of his men commented, "I think . . . the quicker we move now the better."[5] Stuart agreed and ordered the column to move forward at a trot.

Turnstall Station

Later that day, near Turnstall Station, one of Stuart's scouts, John Mosby, was riding ahead of the main

McClellan's army is shown here camped on the Virginia Peninsula, where Stuart's cavalry managed to carry out its successful raid.

column and came across Union cavalry. He was alone and his horse was too tired to make a run for it. Since the Union troopers were not close enough to get a good look at him, Mosby decided to take a chance and resorted to a bluff. He drew his saber, turned his horse around, and waved to the Union horsemen to join him. He hoped they would think he was one of them. They sat in their saddles and watched Mosby for several seconds. Then Stuart's column came into view and they fled.

When the Southern horsemen reached Turnstall Station, they overwhelmed the Union infantry stationed there. Then they harassed a passing train, burned a railroad bridge, and plundered and burned a wagon train.

Although his men were weary, Stuart pushed them on toward the town of Talleysville, five and a half miles away. When they reached the town they found well-stocked Union sutler's stores. Sutlers were peddlers who sold items, often at inflated prices, that the United States government did not provide to soldiers. The hungry Confederate soldiers feasted on figs, beef, tongue, pickles, candy, ketchup, preserves, lemons, cakes, sausages, molasses, crackers, and canned meats.[6]

At 10:00 P.M., Stuart let his men stop to feed their horses and rest for an hour. Then they rode through the night. At 5:00 A.M. on the morning of June 14, they reached the Chickahominy River and found it uncrossable. The banks of the river were swollen due to heavy rains upstream. Stuart's men cut down trees at the river's edge, attempting to make a temporary bridge, but the trees were not long enough and fell into the river.

Stuart knew that the Union Army was on his trail and it would only be a matter of time before it reached him. He sat in his saddle and stroked his beard as he thought. His scouts reported the ruins

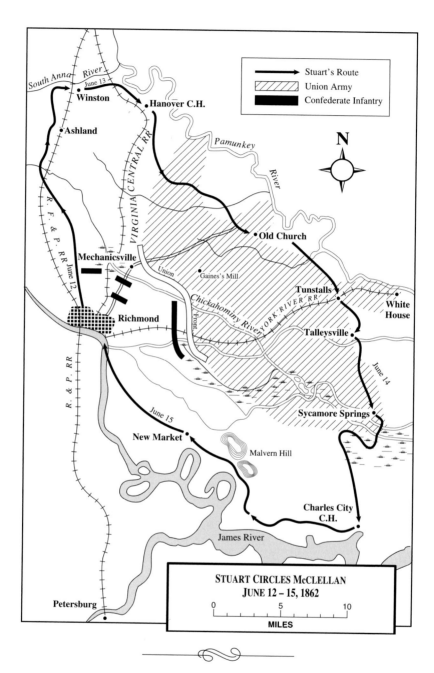

Legend:
- Stuart's Route
- Union Army
- Confederate Infantry

N

South Anna River
June 13
Winston
Hanover C.H.
Ashland
Pamunkey River
R. F. & P. RR June 12
VIRGINIA CENTRAL RR
Old Church
Mechanicsville
Union
Gaines's Mill
Tunstalls
White House
Chickahominy River
YORK RIVER RR
Richmond
Front
Talleysville
R. & P. RR
June 14
June 15
Sycamore Springs
New Market
Malvern Hill
Charles City C.H.
James River
Petersburg

**STUART CIRCLES McCLELLAN
JUNE 12 – 15, 1862**

0   5   10
MILES

In June 1862, Jeb Stuart accomplished an amazing feat when he led his cavalry completely around Union General McClellan's army in only three days. This map shows the route Stuart took on his mission.

of an old bridge a mile away. He examined the bridge and decided to repair it. Two of his men, who had experience building bridges, came forward to rebuild it. An abandoned warehouse provided the necessary wood. The bridge was completed in three hours. By one o'clock that afternoon, the entire column had crossed the river. As the last horsemen set the bridge on fire, a small group of Union cavalry appeared on the other side of the river.

The Confederate troops traveled another seven miles to Charles City Court House before Stuart let his men rest. At dusk he set out with two of his couriers for Richmond, twenty-eight miles away. He left orders for the main column to resume its march at eleven o'clock that evening. During the night Stuart stopped only once for coffee and a few minutes rest. On Sunday morning, June 15, he rode into Richmond and made his report to General Robert E. Lee.

Stuart had achieved an amazing feat. He had ridden nearly one hundred fifty miles in three days, obtained the information he needed, and destroyed or confiscated a considerable amount of Union property. Stuart's raid thoroughly embarrassed the Northern army while raising Southern morale in the process. Overnight, he became a celebrity and hero known as Jeb Stuart, for his first name was replaced by his initials.

2

YOUNG STUART

James Ewell Brown Stuart was the seventh child and youngest son of Archibald Stuart, born December 2, 1795, and Elizabeth Letcher Pannill, born on June 4, 1801. His father was charming, witty, and enjoyed a good time, but his mother had "no special patience with nonsense."[1] Archibald and Elizabeth were married on June 16, 1817, and raised their family on a farm called Laurel Hill in Patrick County, Virginia. Elizabeth had inherited the farm from her grandfather, William Letcher.

Archibald Stuart was a lawyer and elected public official. Because of his profession, he was often away from home. He served one term in the United